SKINNY jeans
FAT shoes

SKINNY jeans FAT shoes

You have the **influence**.
Will you take on the **responsibility**?

Benjamin Gum

SOUL PURPOSE PUBLISHING
Books & Music

Copyright © 2020 Benjamin Gum
All rights reserved.
ISBN 978-1-7344962-4-6

Soul Purpose Publishing
Shawnee, KS

Unless otherwise noted, all Scripture quotations are taken from the Christian Standard Bible®, copyright © 2017 by Holman Bible Publishers. Used by permission. Christian Standard Bible® and CSB® are federally registered trademarks of Holman Bible Publishers.

Contents

ACKNOWLEDGEMENTS VI

DEDICATION VII

INTRODUCTION 1

CHAPTER 1: SEE THE BRAND OF THE SHOES 5

CHAPTER 2: STEP INTO THE SHOES 13

CHAPTER 3: GROW INTO THE SHOES 21

CHAPTER 4: KNEEL IN THE SHOES..31

CHAPTER 5: STAND IN THE SHOES...39

CHAPTER 6: RUN IN THE SHOES...47

CHAPTER 7: CHALLENGE OTHERS WITH THE SHOES................61

Acknowledgements

Thanks to the Father who loved me enough to sacrifice his Son to give me life. Thanks to the Son for taking my sin upon himself and reconciling me to God. Thanks to the Spirit for helping me realize all the riches of God's kindness expressed through Christ, and for granting me stewardship of his spiritual gifts to me. May he work through them to challenge others to faithful stewardship of their own gifts and opportunities.

Thanks to my amazing and supportive wife, Dawna, who is herself my greatest earthly gift. Thanks also to all those family and friends and fellow ministers through whom God has sharpened me over the years, as I have seen and attempted to step into my own pair of fat shoes.

Dedication

In memory of Ron Baker, who wore the shoes well for so many decades as a humble servant.

Introduction

You are already a key influencer. Or you soon will be. Or maybe you are still thinking about it, still deciding. Someone has asked you to lead worship, or maybe you saw a need or opportunity and you offered. Maybe the opportunity is to lead a congregation on a Sunday morning, or perhaps a weekly meeting for a student ministry. Maybe it's for a camp or a conference.

Whatever the ask or the situation looks like, you've probably come to it because you have some musical skill – maybe a LOT of musical skill – or perhaps just enough to go along with your charisma or cool factor to be seen as (the most) qualified to stand in front of people while music happens. You might be mainly a singer. You might have killer guitar or keyboard chops. Maybe you can play ALL the instruments. Maybe you already front a band, or maybe this is your chance to finally do so. Classically trained? Self-taught? Barely know what you're doing?

I've seen all of the above and more in situations where someone was presumably leading worship. More often than not, and more so in recent decades, the people on stage actually are quite skilled musically, and many are pretty charismatic and cool by whatever standards the contemporary culture is measuring cool. This is often especially true of the leader, the one fronting and often, to some degree, directing the band (if there is one). Fact is, if you stand in that role, or you are considering it, it is probably because of your music chops, charisma or cool factor, or all of the above.

That is fine, even appropriate. For a while now, the pop culture of the evangelical church has somewhat lightheartedly adopted a symbol for the person who flourishes onstage in the aforementioned capacities: skinny jeans. We may laugh about it, even spoof it in funny videos, but most worship leaders in exciting, electric or happening churches or events are in fact wearing skinny jeans. Of course, that also reflects styles of the day in general pop culture – or perhaps not so much by the time you read this.

Still, the symbol seems to effectively bring to mind the person who steps on stage with a certain amount of presence and persona.

My purpose with this book is not to disparage worship leaders from being stylish or cool or culturally relevant. In fact, I think in their proper places these things are helpful. The last one, being culturally relevant, is actually an ongoing demand upon any local church that intends to transfer faith from one generation to the next. This amounts to what the missiologist calls *contextualization*. I'm all for that. In fact, I've spent a good part of my ministry years and effort helping churches regain or maintain good contextualization.

My purpose is not to condemn or replace skinny jeans or what they symbolize. I even have skinny jeans of my own (relatively speaking ... okay, *very* relatively speaking). My purpose is to call you to MORE. If you are a worship leader in some stage role, you already have a platform and you already have influence – perhaps more than you realize. I want to show you that you also have *responsibility*. You may not want it, but if you stand before people with the presumed task of leading – or even simply facilitating – worship of the one true God, then you have responsibility.

To explore that responsibility, I will use another symbol: shoes. More specifically, big FAT shoes. As in the old saying, "You have some big shoes to fill." However it is that you come to the stage, whatever your capacities, I want you to first realize that the shoes are there waiting for you. They are there by nature of the position, and they demand a response. You will either acknowledge them and embrace the responsibility, or you will ignore them and shy away from the responsibility. That doesn't make them – or it – go away.

Skinny jeans may bring you to the stage, and they represent the influence you do in fact have. It is the shoes that characterize what you *do* with that influence. One must submit to the other. If the skinny jeans rule, then top priority goes to influence for its own sake. Cultural relevance becomes king, and celebrity is its court. Songs and styles will be defined by

Introduction

how they sound, how they feel, how the crowd responds. The worshipers may find themselves at a dessert buffet, feasting on whipped topping but receiving little or no nourishment for their souls. Their spiritual energy for the week will be spent in about 90 hyperactive minutes on Sunday morning, followed by a six-day crash.

On the other hand, if the shoes rule, all the other considerations are grounded and submitted to what God has revealed that he desires from his worshipers. Relevance and cultural trappings have their place, but they are submitted to the responsible handling of this opportunity to feed and fellowship. Souls are nourished, spiritual gifts are expressed in love, and there is still room for dessert. Gospel energy will sustain through the week (along with daily feedings).

My desire is to see you – and a whole generation of worship leaders – step into the fat shoes, even while you thrive in your skinny jeans. The come-and-go nature of the skinny jeans – if those are all you concern yourself with – will lead you down a road fraught with empty pursuit, like the Teacher's chasing after smoke in Ecclesiastes. However, if you are willing to step into and grow into the fat shoes of responsible leadership, you will find that it is perpetually rewarding.

I do not mean to overwhelm you. You may have never given this stuff a thought, or you might be just now getting your feet wet in this corporate worship stuff and you're just trying to keep your head above water. I mean to plant some seeds, and to get you to take the first step. Step into the shoes. As with most Christian things, the order gets reversed. Going forward, before you pull on the jeans, put on the shoes. They are hugely oversized – trust me. Don't sweat that. Just lace them up. Unlike regular shoes they won't conform to *your* shape, but rather the *opposite*. They will begin to grow you into a leader shaped by the gospel. They will bring you to your knees, and that's a good thing. You will begin to see yourself as a servant. This is most appropriate, for the shoes belong to the Suffering Servant who gave you all your chops, and who brought you into this moment. Regardless of how you see yourself, the Father sees you with Jesus. If you will walk with him in these shoes, others will see Jesus too.

You've already stepped into the jeans. You have influence. The stage will magnify that. Now, will you step into the shoes? Will you grow into the responsibility God has given you? If not, please walk away from the stage, at least THIS stage. Be a performer or public speaker in some environment other than that of corporate worship, but don't stand in front of the church. (By the way, there are similar shoes for Christians in those other environments, too.) It is my prayer that you *will* accept the challenge. I can say from experience that it is worth it. Step into the shoes and see where God takes you. If you will, I want to help, so please read on.

Chapter 1: See the Brand of the Shoes

What kinds of shoes do you prefer? What fills the floor of your closet? Slip-on casual? Lace-up ankle boots? Leather? Canvas? What brands and styles? Chucks? Toms? Jordans?

Back in my teen years, I was partial to Nike, preferring low cut basketball shoes (I never spent the bucks for Jordans). As an adult, I came to prefer Adidas running shoes for everyday use and for some of the sports I played. I still liked the low-cut Nikes for basketball, though, and still do today. Nowadays my range of shoes includes some Nike runners, some Sambas, a pair of casual canvas Adidas, some slip-on Sketchers, some leather ankle-boots, some stylish dress blacks (mostly for weddings and funerals) and some Timberlines. My wife helps me not look like a dork, while I operate mainly on what fits me comfortably. That's the main function of any brand loyalty for me – I tend to stick with what fits me well.

How about you? What drove the choices sitting in your closet? Style at any cost? Are you someone who will wear shoes that look good even if they kill you? Are you more inclined to wear a pair of raggedy, worn-out old shoes that are just too comfortable to trash, though you probably should have thrown them out years ago? Do you have a favorite brand or style that always seems to fit you well?

I challenge you to consider the brand of your worship-leader shoes. Not your actual shoes but these metaphorical shoes that symbolize your responsibility. You get to pick your actual shoes based on any number of your own preferences, but these worship-leader shoes are not like that. They come in only one brand. They might be said to be available in various *styles* – if we think in terms of contextualization that I mentioned in the introduction – but they come in only one *brand*. There are no acceptable knock-offs, those cheap superstore versions styled to imitate the real deal. I say "acceptable" because there *are* knock-offs, but they are not acceptable replacements. Avoid those shoes and stick with real worship-leader shoes. One brand. What is the brand for these worship-leader shoes?

The gospel. These are gospel shoes. The brand is not your own, not your band's, not even your local church's. It is the gospel of Jesus Christ. You may write and record your own worship songs. Your church may grow its brand to achieve regional, national or even international recognition. But neither you nor your church defines the true gospel. Not even the prolific Apostle Paul, who penned much of what the New Testament says about the gospel, claimed to do that. He made it very clear that the gospel was only something he *received* (Galatians 1:12), *preached* (v.23), *presented* (2:2) *and preserved* (v.5). In fact, Paul pronounced a curse on anyone – even an angel! – who might preach a knock-off gospel (1:6-9). We don't define the gospel brand. We only *deliver* it, as Jude, the half-brother of Jesus, said (Jude v.3). We display it. We show it off and celebrate it.

We either deliver the true gospel, or we deliver a knock-off. When you step onstage, you are preaching a gospel, either a true one or a false one. You are either wearing real Chucks or you are wearing one of the many canvas "lawsuit" knock-offs sold in stores like Kmart or Walmart.

Don't take the stage in your church wearing gospel knock-offs. The potential results are far more important than any kind of social *faux pas*. They may include confusion, false security and even eternal damnation! Sadly, as important as this is, many before you will not be able to tell whether you are wearing the real deal or the counterfeit, whether you are standing in the true gospel or a false one. You may yourself not be much of an expert on telling the true gospel shoes from the knock-offs. In truth, a core reason the church gathers is to rehearse over and over what the true gospel is, so that we may all be inoculated against believing a false gospel.

That's why putting on the right shoes is so important for *you*. The *crowd* is far too willing to take the worship leader's word for it. They are sheep. They'll tend to wander wherever there seems to be grass for eating, never mind the cliffs or the wolves or the thieves. They need some shepherding. Now, you might say, "Hey, isn't that why we have pastors?" You'd be right. Unless you hold a position like Worship *Pastor*, you are probably not charged with spiritual oversight of the church like pastors are, but that does not mean that you are not responsible to function like a shepherd when you take the stage to lead worship. In the next chapter, I will argue that you are responsible for *exactly* that, at least to some degree, as you safeguard the gospel that is getting rehearsed by the sheep.

For now, if you will grant my premise that we must see our worship-leader shoes as gospel shoes, and if you will also grant that we must ensure they are branded by the real gospel and not knock-offs, let us inspect what the real deal looks like. What is the true gospel?

The term "gospel" means "good news." It is a particular good news, and its realization was anticipated for millennia. Most biblical scholars see the earliest seed form of this good news back in Genesis 3:15, where God promises *a descendant of the first human couple would deliver a lethal blow to the head of the serpent* who fooled mankind into rebelling against God and falling out of his favor. This victory by that future Human would come at a cost, though, as he would suffer a lethal bite to his heel. Still, here in the curse that resulted from man's Fall there is hope of good news.

As history looks for this Man, God approaches a man named Abram and tells him he is going to bring blessing to all the peoples of mankind through one of his descendants (Genesis 12:1-3). The good news comes into sharper focus. *The Man who will defeat the serpent will be a descendant of Abram (now called Abraham) and will bring blessing to mankind.* This promise gets repeated to Isaac and Jacob, Abraham's son and grandson.

At one point, God has worked it so that one of Jacob's sons is second only to Pharaoh in Egypt. A huge famine brings all of the family there where God provides for them. When Jacob is on his deathbed, he pronounces what will happen to all his twelve sons. When he comes to

Judah he says, "The scepter will not depart from Judah or the staff from between his feet until he whose right it is comes and the obedience of the peoples belongs to him" (Genesis 49:10). So, *the Man of the good news will come from Judah's descendants.*

Many years later, Abraham's descendants have grown to a nation of a couple million. They are discouraged by centuries of enslavement in Egypt, in desperate need of the good news. God miraculously saves them through a series of events that culminates in a night called the Passover. In that night every firstborn son died throughout all the land unless the household was covered by blood from a sacrificial lamb. This event was core to the worshiping community of God's people, for God commanded them to celebrate the Passover rescue every year. Now we are looking for *a Man who will bring blessing through being sacrificed like a lamb.*

Years later we get a bizarre update in the timing of the good news expectation. It is bizarre in that it comes from a soothsayer, a diviner named Balaam, who actually wanted desperately to curse God's people rather than bless them. (To do so was going to make him very rich!) God didn't allow that. (There was a talking donkey involved. I told you it was bizarre.) God ends up speaking through Balaam who says (in Numbers 24:17), "I see him, but not now; I perceive him, but not near. A star will come from Jacob, and a scepter will arise from Israel." He goes on to announce that this leader will destroy Israel's enemies. So, this Man for whom we are looking – who will defeat the serpent, who will bring blessing through suffering, who will come from the tribe of Judah – *this man will come as a powerful ruler, but not now.* He will come, but in Balaam's time he is not yet near.

Throughout the rest of the Old Testament the promise of the good news continues to be accompanied by waiting. In the meantime, God's people, the Israelites (and all others who come to worship YHWH) repeatedly rebel against God, echoing the rebellion in the Garden of Eden, and eventually acting even WORSE than the pagan nations around them.

In response to this history of failure, God speaks through his prophets to show us the most important aspects of the good news. *God is going to give his people a new heart* (Ezekiel 11:19 and 36:26). *He himself is going to pay for all of his people's failures and sins through his Servant* (Isaiah 53). This Servant will suffer all the shame and wrath that humans deserve, and in exchange will provide satisfaction, justice and peace.

So, as we approach the first century, the good news tells us we are looking for *a Man descended from Abraham, from the tribe of Judah, sent by God as a substitute to take all the wrath we deserve because of our sinful rebellion. He'll be a Man who will suffer in our place to satisfy God, to justify us before him, to provide peace for us, to give us new hearts willing to obey God, and to establish eternal blessing for God's people from every nation.* That's the good news of promise from God.

Then Jesus came. Everything the Old Testament taught us to look for was fulfilled perfectly in him. Now the Man has a name. Jesus suffered like the lamb of the Passover, but his slaughter provided the once-for-all payment for all sins. He took our place of condemnation and took God's wrath. He crushed the serpent's head. He gave those who trust him new hearts, new life. He raised from the dead to show himself the victorious ruler over all. He accomplished all this because he is God himself. The gospel is the good news of Jesus and his finished work. The Fourfold Gospel of Matthew, Mark, Luke and John brilliantly displays the way Jesus epitomizes the good news.

My favorite short version of the gospel comes from Paul in 1 Corinthians 15:3-4: "**... that Christ died for our sins according to the Scriptures, that he was buried, that he was raised on the third day according to the Scriptures ...**" In these three phrases we get the essentials, though Paul spent thousands of words exploring and explaining various aspects of the good news.

Here we see our need, that sins require a death. There is no need for or rejoicing in good news unless there was first bad news. The bad news of the Fall, our inherited sinfulness, and our own deliberate sin and its consequences was the worst possible news – eternal damnation and separation from God. Christ died and was buried for us, to pay for our sins.

We see the authentication of the means and Man of our rescue. God has spoken. Jesus was appointed to save us, and his appointment was revealed in the Scriptures. His mission was predicted and authenticated by the Scriptures. His victory was spelled out and celebrated by the Scriptures.

We see the power and life of the resurrected Lord who was first Creator and Source of life. After his brief obedient humiliation, Jesus was vindicated by resurrection and exalted once again to his rightful position as worthy of all worship. His work and glory continue to be expressed in those he raises to life in himself, those who believe and live according to this good news.

Of course, the gospel is a subject that we will explore and celebrate for all eternity. It is far too complex to contemplate in full detail, whether in a book, or a series of books, or a worship service or a thousand worship services. That's actually a beautiful reality for you and me when we take the stage to lead a community of worshipers. The object and subject of our worship – Jesus and his work of salvation – are inexhaustible. Gospel-centered worship need never be stale or boring. We can and will be forever exercising our creativity to articulate and celebrate the gospel.

But our creativity must never carry our focus off Jesus and his work. The gospel is bigger than big, but it does have identifiable themes. We acknowledge our great need (because of our sin). We humbly confess our sin and our complete dependence upon God's provision and mercy. We are assured of pardon through faith in the completed work of Christ upon the cross. We understand the penal substitutionary atonement for sin, that Jesus took our place to bear God's righteous wrath and gives us a righteous standing through our union with him. We recognize the work of the Holy Spirit to draw, to awaken and make us alive. We celebrate the power to obey and follow Christ as those who possess his eternal life. We give thanks for God's provision and unmerited favor. We celebrate victory in Christ over sin and death. We realize and acknowledge that our mission is to bear witness to these truths before the world.

The list goes on and on, of course, and can be expressed in many different ways. For help in identifying core themes that ought to find regular feature in your worship, I encourage you to do a little research into liturgies that have guided gospel-focused worship over the centuries. If you serve in a church adhering to Reformed traditions, you may well have a sort of liturgical template in place for you. In that case, your task would be to ensure your songs, or readings or prayers were faithfully reflecting each particular gospel theme. You may well be in a more free-church environment, where much or all of these elements are left to your discretion. Even if you don't hold to a particular template, I encourage you to map out various gospel themes and find rhythms that ensure you are balanced in your services and over the long haul.

Many times, you will find that an upcoming preaching text will suggest an emphasis on certain gospel themes, and I would encourage you to make it a regular habit to consider that in your planning. For my part, though, over the years I have softened some on that priority. I now seek a balance of gospel themes as my highest priority (though I am not as strict or formal as a high church liturgist). I do always think through the preaching text, and whenever a solid song or reading comes to mind that coheres with the thrust of that text, I will certainly use it. I do not, however, normally express only one particular theme throughout the service. I will seek to balance out a handful of gospel themes through the other songs, or at least through other liturgical elements.

However we come to approach it, we must stay aware of and anchored to these many gospel themes, and we must keep the God who saves at the center of our worship. If we do not, we will quickly and easily slip into a false gospel. We will find ourselves thinking things about ourselves that are only true about God. We will still be worshiping, but we will not be honoring the only one worthy of worship. He is seeking people who will worship him in spirit and truth (John 4:23, ESV). The gospel is our tractor beam. If we get caught in the gravitational pull of any worldly counterfeit and drift off, our worship is not in truth, and it is unacceptable to God.

Put on the right shoes. Wear them carefully. The true gospel of Jesus Christ is our brand. We stand in that. No matter what logo is on the projection screen, we stand in the gospel. We worship Jesus. No matter who we are, no matter who is in the crowd, no matter who else is involved, we worship Jesus. His gospel is our brand. Put on his shoes or please stay out of leadership. Serve in the band or stay in the crowd, but don't lead gathered worship unless you will wear authentic gospel shoes.

Chapter 2: Step into the Shoes

If you found the previous chapter intimidating at all, then I have succeeded so far. There is a certain gravity one should feel when he or she steps into any position of leadership in the church. This is even more true for those of us who are in what are arguably the two most influential roles in our congregations (the other being the preacher/teacher). I am so grateful that I learned to feel that gravity from pastors under which and alongside which I have served. Sadly, many church leaders do not focus as much attention on the responsibility borne by the worship leaders as they do on the preachers. Worse than that, many preachers today don't even feel this gravity themselves. I believe both they and the worship leaders *must* feel it, because the leaders in these two positions carry out different expressions of the same function of teaching. I'll explain that more in a moment. For now, let me reassert that we must feel the weight of our responsibility as worship leaders.

Having said that, it is not my goal to chase you off from this great opportunity. Quite the opposite, I want to encourage you to bear the weight I hope you now feel. Like the good feeling after a hard day's work, there is a reward for shouldering well this burden. Put on the shoes. Lace them up and commit to the responsibility of rightly handling the true gospel. *Feel and accept the weight of putting words in the mouths and hearts of your people.*

Do you realize that you do both of those things when you plan out a worship set list? You are choosing the words that your congregants will sing. Those words have meaning, and they communicate something to the mind and soul. They will either draw them to understand, reflect upon, believe, and celebrate the true gospel or a false one. You cannot control how they respond to the truths communicated by the words, but you are in control of what words and truths to which they must respond. For this very reason, it may be that you are submitted to a process where a pastor signs off on your selections. If so, that is a good thing. Be encouraged that a pastor wants to help you shoulder the load well. If you are not asked to do so, I suggest you proactively reach out in advance to the teaching pastor and discuss your song choices whenever possible. Most will (and should) welcome this, even if they do not direct you to make any changes. Your planning will have an impact similar to his. In fact, the impact of the song selections may be even greater.

The pastor/teacher will (if he is faithful) expose the gospel directly from the biblical text. In today's Western setting, he will prepare and deliver theology through a centuries-old rhetorical style where he speaks and the congregation listens. This is crucial, and it is a gospel meal. However, this gospel rehearsal is almost exclusively one-sided communication. Hopefully, the listeners are *active* listeners.

Wise worship service planners work hard to provide several strategic opportunities for interaction through responsive reading, the giving of gifts during the offering, the participation in the Lord's Table, and the like. This is where the worship leaders (by which I mean the ones fronting the band and especially if they plan the songs) have an advantage. The theological material they use (and it is that) will involve a high degree of congregational interaction. At least it should. The congregants will not only be listening but singing. They will often be standing, perhaps raising their hands or even dancing or jumping (easy, easy, now!). The point is that while during the *preaching* theology is hitting the brain and, hopefully, the heart, during the *singing* theology is being cemented in the whole person. This is a great opportunity for impact – either responsibly with the true gospel or irresponsibly with a false gospel.

Think about it. How many sermons can you remember? Not whole sermons – give me a break! – just the main ideas of the sermons. I'll be honest, I've preached quite a few sermons, and off-hand I could probably recall the main thrust of only a few – that I preached! That doesn't mean they weren't effective. As a pastor friend of mine often says, I don't remember too many meals, but you can look at me and easily tell that those meals kept me nourished. How many of your spiritual meals do you remember (in terms of sermons)? Probably not too many.

How many songs do you know? To be fair, let's keep comparing apples to apples. How many *church* songs do you know? If you've been around the church for very long, you may only remember a sermon or two, but you probably already know dozens of congregational worship songs. You could probably sing some of them with your eyes closed (i.e., from memory). You probably know even more Christian songs that you may not sing in church. These songs are sources for spiritual meals too. These meals probably have as much or more to do with what you believe about God as those sermons do. Remember, even though a 30 to 40-minute sermon may have a greater sheer quantity of biblical content and more technical information, the theological content of the songs we sing in church is being imbedded by the repeated interaction of our whole persons. If the pastor preaches that sermon again in a few weeks, he might get pushback, but we won't think twice about singing the same song again. Nor should we, at least in the case of good songs. The messages of our songs are being driven deep and being reinforced by repetition.

This happens outside the church as well. I remember when I was in junior high that we had a jukebox in our public-school lunchroom. (Okay. A juke-box was a large box full of vinyl records holding popular song recordings of the day. One would put coin money – you've heard of that? – into a slot and then select a Top 40 hit to play. Google it, if you must.) Now, this wasn't the 50's but rather the 80's. So, I make no exaggeration – I actually counted at one point – on a daily basis I would hear two songs as many as seven times: Back in Black by AC/DC and More Than A Feeling by Boston. Those two songs imbedded in my soul a familiarity and affinity for the musical style of that day.

Now, I am a classically trained double-bass player and singer who over the last 40 years has picked up keyboards, electric bass, guitars and a little skill on drums. So, I appreciate pretty much every style of music. Still, largely due to that jukebox I have a special affinity for 80's rock (give or take a decade). More to the point, I realize I had a lot of exposure to the lyrical themes of songs that were popular during those times. The musical vehicle is the hook, but there are messages inside. I don't know how many times I have heard a classic come up over restaurant speakers, begun to follow along in my head (or even out loud), and then stopped short when I realized the lyric was offensive to my decades-older biblical sensibilities. I still love the music, but I have become aware of the dangers of ungodly lyrics. Not a song prude, but aware and cautious.

That's why you need to put on the shoes. The congregation is like you and me. They walk around with little snippets of false gospels in their heads and hearts. They've picked these bits up from home, school, the workplace, the gym, from social media, from entertainment – *especially* from entertainment! – from all kinds of sources. When they gather with the church, they desperately need to rehearse the true gospel in the songs that are selected. Selected by *you*, I presume. If not by you, then likely by someone with whom you have influence.

Worship leaders are accountable, then, for at least a couple of reasons. First, God doesn't mess around with leaders who mess around when it comes to worship and his holiness. Remember Nadab and Abihu? God was just beginning to help his people understand his holiness and how important it was to approach him carefully in worship. In Exodus 25-31 God had given Moses his law to explain how his people should honor him. Before Moses got down from the mountain, they were worshiping a golden calf! Clearly, they needed help with understanding proper worship.

God had given clear instructions, and had appointed Aaron's sons, including Nadab and Abihu, to serve as priests with special privileges to draw near to God on behalf of his people while they worshiped holding their distance. They had gone through this special ceremony for appointment and for cleansing to serve as worship leaders. The glory of the LORD appeared to Israel. It was a big deal. "Great worship today, Moses!" Then, the next thing recorded in the text, Leviticus 10:1-3, these two guys screwed it up. They approached the LORD with "unauthorized fire, which he had not commanded them to do." It's not exactly clear what their offense was, but the point is that they blew off God to do their own thing. He consumed them with fire, and they died "before the LORD."

I think that last phrase from verse two is telling. As worship leaders (or any other kind of leader) in the church, we are accountable *before the Lord*, and he is holy. I haven't personally known any worship leaders, even the worst of them, to be consumed by fire for screwing up – that is God's grace – but that doesn't mean he doesn't still take leadership just as seriously as he did then. Take that to heart.

There is another reason worship leaders are accountable. It relates to the teaching function of corporate worship. I'm not talking about the preacher. I'm talking about the whole congregation. Paul says in Colossians 3:16 that when Christians gather to sing in worship, they are "teaching and admonishing one another in all wisdom." Admonishing means to warn or counsel someone about how to behave. Paul takes a different angle when he talks about congregational singing in Ephesians 5:19, but there too he talks about how it is to cause wise, Spirit-filled living. Do you see the connection? When the church sings together, they are teaching each other how to live. There's gravity to that. James, the half-brother of Jesus and leader of the large church in Jerusalem in the first century, cautioned people who wanted teaching positions, saying they "will receive a stricter judgment." While most are not in a teaching position per se, when the congregation sings, they are *functioning* like teachers.

Do you see why it is a big deal that you are putting words in their mouths? The people singing those songs you pick out are teaching each other how to live. They are either teaching themselves to live by the true gospel or by a false one. If you pick your church's songs, you are effectively picking curriculum for the largest class. I think the case can be made that when the worship leader is selecting songs, he or she is standing in a teaching role, and according to James, is held to a higher accountability than the rest of the congregation. You and I are helping our people indoctrinate each other, and I believe God holds us accountable for that responsibility.

I know very well the kinds of concerns that typically dominate our Sunday preparation as worship leaders. *What songs will work well with my personnel this week? What keys will work best for the singers, for the guitarists, for the congregation? What order will flow right, give us a lift as we go? Have I mixed up tempos and grooves enough? Can my electric guitarist play that lead lick? Do I need to refine any charts?*

Please understand, these are valid concerns that you do need to think through. In fact, I will address them later on, and give my take on some practical tips that have come to me over the years. But I don't think these are the questions God will ask when you and I give account to him for our ministries to our local congregations. I think he will ask what we were putting in the mouths of our congregants to instruct and encourage one another. *Were we giving them a diet rich in gospel? Was it filled with the meaty truths of Scripture, or fast-fading feel-good carbs? Did they taste the true sweetness of God's goodness, or were we filling them up on artificial, highly processed sweeteners? Were we nourishing the body or only teasing the tongue? Did the meals we set sustain our people, or only prop them up with a brief rush, only to be followed by a week-long crash?*

Make no mistake. If you have been granted the influence, you *will* answer for how you handled it. We all know the feeling of an upcoming exam. How different do we feel if we are *well* prepared for that exam versus if we are *not* prepared? It is better that we examine *ourselves* with these questions rather than to be judged and disciplined by the Lord (1 Corinthians 11:28-32). If we take our responsibility seriously and prayerfully, we will not have to fear or be ashamed when God evaluates our stewardship of the influence he gave us.

Step into the Shoes

So, I encourage you to accept the call. Step into the shoes. Take on this responsibility to love your church people well and to help them nourish each other on the rich and sustaining food of the true gospel. Look seriously at the content of the worship songs, readings and other elements you incorporate into your worship gatherings and do your best to help implant the gospel deep into the souls of your brothers and sisters in Christ.

Chapter 3: Grow into the Shoes

I have challenged you to take on the responsibility of being a leader who helps your church people know, believe and live in the true gospel. Your decision to do so has an ongoing impact on them, but it also will continue to impact you. I want you to not only be aware of this but to aggressively pursue it. I want you to grow into the shoes.

I have to add a caveat right away, and I foreshadowed it earlier when I said that Jesus and his work, as the subject and object of our worship, are inexhaustible. That is, the challenge to grow into these gospel shoes is a direction, a trend more than a destination or endpoint. The shoes will never stop being too big. That does not mean it is okay to not grow. Rather, we should never stop growing in the gospel. It is far more than a gateway to Christian life. It is the sustaining *reality* of Christian life.

Let these gospel shoes shape you and grow you and let them shape and grow a gospel culture around you. This can and should happen in many informal, organic ways. As is often said, the gospel is simple enough for a child to understand. Because of this, gospel growth is accessible to any believer, yourself included.

I challenge you to go farther. Commit to be a learner. Learn every way you can. Let me be clear that among the options I am referring to learning from your peers, learning from mentors, learning from reading (ugh! I know), from podcasts, and even from formal training (e.g., Bible College or seminary), if you have not already had any.

I am staggered by the difference 30+ years has made in my approach to leading worship (I started *extremely* young!). It seems to me that my progress was greatly accelerated by two key factors that I especially commend to you: mentorship and pursuit of formal studies. As with many things in life, in worship leading (the robust kind with which I am challenging you) we are likely to find that just as we start to feel like we have a handle on how to go about it, we realize we may not have too many years left to practice what we have learned. It is my goal to encourage you to aggressively pursue your growth early on so that you may be highly effective in ministry even as you continue to grow into the shoes. This will put you in a situation much like Paul described to Timothy, the young pastor he was mentoring. Paul gave Timothy a bunch of instructions and then in 1 Timothy 4:15 he told his protégé, "Practice these things; be committed to them, so that your progress may be evident to all." He explained that as Timothy pursued his own growth it would save both himself and the people he led. The same will be true with you as you seek to grow into your gospel shoes. So, let me speak more practically about these ways to grow.

One of the most important things you can do is to draw from those who have done this before you and longer than you, and from those who do it in different contexts. I remember when I was learning to play sports, how much I picked up by watching others, seeing what worked for them and emulating their techniques. I learned not only what *worked* but also what was *allowed*. I played a fair amount of volleyball before I learned from my wife that I was often "carrying" the ball, using techniques that were not allowed in official play. I remember learning in basketball that I was in fact fowling other players left and right. So, early on I was learning what was "okay" and what was not. Many years later, I still notice what an opposing guard does to foil my defense, and I try to figure out if and how I can make that technique work for myself. I often joke with my son when he torches me on the court, "You got that move from me!" I hope it's true (though these days the age gap is probably a bigger factor), because I want him to be a learner. I want that for you too.

There's a good chance you play an instrument. If so, you've probably spent a good deal of time watching videos online to figure out how an artist is playing a song you want to use. What fingering shape are they using on guitar? What capo key? How did they play that lick? I remember wondering what on earth possessed a worship band to pick the key of Db major for a particular song and then realizing that this key put the main piano riff on all black keys. I remember learning from my electric guitar player what an EBow is. How long did I struggle with acoustic guitar before I discovered most rhythm players were using capos rather than barre chords? How many years did I play electric bass before I discovered the art of playing the same pitch on a different string to get a different timbre, energy and sustain?

I don't envy the worship leader who ever notices me in the crowd, because I imagine I am not very inspiring. I'm not the guy dancing around with a bunch of energy. I'm usually staring at one of the band members, trying to figure out what gear he's using or what drove his choices about how to play that riff he's playing. That's got to be a lot more fun for me than for the person who happens to watch me watch someone else.

I have not only learned in these informal ways from others, but in more formal ones too. I came up classically trained as a double bass player in the orchestral setting and crossed over into jazz at the collegiate level. I studied voice as a music major. I've attended worship leading conferences and songwriting classes. There are many formal ways for someone to grow as an artist, including not only the collegiate environment but private instruction, online classes and seminars and more. We should grab every kind of opportunity to grow in these ways.

I love to learn. I want you to love learning too. There's a pretty good chance you are already compelled as I am to learn as an artist. Perhaps you've spent a few thousand hours learning from the great ones on your particular instrument, or maybe you spent years in choirs and under voice coaches to get better at singing. Keep learning as a musician and artist.

But my challenge to grow into the shoes is about more than growing as an artist. *You need to grow theologically.* You need to continually grow in your awareness of and understanding of gospel themes. As with your artistic growth, you can learn theology both informally and formally, and you can learn broadly from the crowd of many skilled experts as well as more specifically from a particular mentor. Take advantage of all the options. In particular, though, I challenge you to look for any opportunity to pursue formal theological training and I encourage you to sit under a capable theological mentor.

There are many places that offer excellent undergraduate and graduate instruction in music and other performance arts, but to get solid Bible training beyond the church setting you need to look to Bible colleges and seminaries. You might be surprised at the quality of music education that can be found in many of these theologically-oriented institutions, and if you wish to pursue both advanced musical training and theological training there are good options. However, if you, like many worship leaders today, are already proficient as a musician, the options for pursuing purely biblical/theological training are many and diverse. There has been an explosion of online offerings that give you the ability to select among the best colleges and seminaries without the need to move to a campus or even to disrupt your schedule. Still, if you are wired more to benefit from an in-person campus learning environment, there is almost surely a solid Bible college or seminary near you. If you have never had formal theological training, I urge you to find one of these solid institutions and pursue advanced training in whatever format suits you best. If you eagerly dig into these studies, I have no doubt you will experience gospel growth in a matter of months that would likely have taken you years or decades to realize otherwise.

A solid theological institution is going to be built on and training you for solid biblical interpretive method. It will be rock solid on core biblical issues: things that have been for two millennia recognized by the church as essential for salvation and for orthodoxy. Many institutions (especially some more targeted on the arts than on sound theology) will focus on secondary or even tertiary theological issues to the extent that they compromise on primary ones. Avoid these, even if you agree with them about those non-essential positions. The point is whether or not they help you understand and grow in core gospel issues, and they (and you) will succeed or fail there based on being saturated with Scripture and applying sound and effective interpretive skills. That is, you should look for training somewhere that will both immerse you in the Bible AND train you well in properly interpreting it.

This kind of training (if you are diligent) will do some unique things for you. You will take in and reflect upon big chunks of Scripture in short periods of time, like you probably have not done before. Even after decades of church instruction and my own study and teaching, I was amazed at how much better a sense of the big picture I got of a passage, a biblical book or even the whole Bible. You'll probably find the same. You will become more aware of the continuity, diversity and genius of God's revelation through the most amazing literary work of all time. You should certainly come across verses, phrases or ideas that you realize you have totally misunderstood because you have passively acquired your interpretations from anywhere but careful study of the Bible. (I like the term "folk theologies" to describe these ideas.) In many other cases you will find you had an essentially correct understanding of a doctrine, but you will come to understand it in far more precision and detail. You will be exposed to arguments for and against the common theological positions regarding major doctrines. You will interact with instructors and other students to challenge your thinking and to critically evaluate those positions. The experience should have ironic results. You should increase in your understanding and confidence about foundational doctrines while at the same time deepening in your humility and open-handedness about non-essential ones. You will know the truth better while realizing more and more how much you do not know.

Above all else, if you pursue the kind of theological training about which I write, you will come to know Christ more deeply. This is not about merely accumulating knowledge, for thinking we have things all figured out is what the Apostle Paul says will puff us up with pride (1 Corinthians

8:1). This is about passionate learning that leads us to love. Our diligent Bible study causes us to see and love Jesus more fervently, and when that happens, we come to love others in a way that "builds them up" as Paul says. Growing into these gospel shoes means coming to know the good news more precisely and fully, but especially it means coming to know the Savior more deeply. This is crucial for us as worship leaders, because, as I said before, we are helping them teach one another. More than that, we are helping them see Christ. As a worship leader, the more you know and see the truth, the more you know and see Christ, the more you can help the congregation do the same. So, grow in this. Go after this with theological training.

Of course, it is possible for you to grow – even in the ways described above – without formal training. It is possible for you to hunger after the Word, to consume it and study it. You can accumulate resources that help you learn to rightly understand and teach the word of truth, just as Paul instructed Timothy to do in 2 Timothy 2:15. You already have the one essential resource itself in the Bible. You have the Holy Spirit, and the expectation of God's help when you pray for understanding as you study the Bible. There are many tools today for you to pursue growth on your own. However, God has designed a community as a key learning context for the follower of Christ, and he has done so for important reasons. He knows we need accountability, not only to spur us to learn and grow but also to check and inform our conclusions as we do so. He knows we need one another to be able to put good doctrine (orthodoxy) into good practice (orthopraxy). The primary community for this learning and loving is the church. Still, beyond that, Bible colleges and seminaries offer a more intensive and carefully guided environment that is extremely useful to take disciples farther faster in biblical training than the typical congregational setting.

I myself began to feel the need for formalized theological training when I was well into my thirties and nearly two decades into church leadership. I felt the weight of being a gospel minister like I hadn't before, even though I only occasionally preached and was not at the time even holding a pastoral office (I was Worship Director). I began with a college level video theological program that was very helpful. That whetted an appetite in me that was eventually only satisfied (to this point) with my completion of undergraduate and graduate degrees in theological studies. Your path may be very different from mine, but that is not the point. I want you to get started on it sooner than I did, and I hope to help you feel the weight of the responsibility sooner than I did. Whether you are led to a formal setting or not, I urge you to go after the kind of intense learning about which I have written to promote your own growth.

Paul and Timothy illustrate another key targeted method for growing into these gospel shoes. I highly recommend that you to seek out a mentor. A mentoring relationship too can be formal or informal. As with academic learning, I think there is a benefit to some degree of formalized mentoring. You may certainly learn from any number of seasoned (worship) leaders by observing them directly or via blogs, articles, videos and the like. They may not even know you or be aware that you look to them for guidance or tips. As I mentioned earlier, I do recommend learning from others in these ways. Still, it is my experience that you will have even more to gain if there is someone you can approach and sit under who is capable and willing to show you how things are done well. Find a worship leader as near your context as possible (hopefully in your own church), who can save you from repeating their past mistakes, encourage you in best practices and help you think maturely and wisely through issues that may be new to both of you. Ideally, this person is someone who can start by letting you watch while they carry the leadership responsibilities (like with internships), can walk beside you as they gradually give you more and more of your own responsibilities, and then who will support you as leadership is handed to you.

Learning things the hard way through our own experiences may be effective but it is not as *efficient* as guided learning with a mentor. I remember I was in my teens when our worship pastor gave me a limited responsibility. In those days we always finished our services with an "altar call." This meant that the congregation would sing while our pastors were available for counseling any who came down front for spiritual help. This pastor was primarily responsible for music, but wanted to be free to counsel, so he asked me to lead the singing during this time. As the preacher winded down (I was very familiar with his preaching rhythms), I would consider the focus of his message, think through the 15 or 20 appropriate response songs in our hymnal and write down a number on a piece of paper. Then I would hand the paper to our pianist/organist who was meeting me on stage as the teaching pastor prayed. No biggie. I knew the songs (and the hymnal numbers) by heart, and merely led the congregation in singing. This little responsibility gave me shoes into which to grow, freed a pastor for other tasks, and served our congregation. It wasn't long before I was in another, smaller church directing all the music. That kind of initial step in handing off responsibility was something a mentor does, though that pastor and I never formalized such a relationship.

In fact, no one ever formally took me under his wing in the way I am recommending for you. To be fair, neither did I go asking anyone to do so. I didn't realize until recent years how beneficial that would have been. God has always been faithful to me, but as I look back now over 30 years into church leadership, I wonder how much better I might have served and led in my churches if I had been directly mentored all those years ago. It is only by God's grace that I was effective to the extent I was, which, of course, would be true had I been formally mentored as well.

I want to be clear as I close this chapter on growing into the shoes. When I look back wondering what impact formal training and deliberate mentoring might have had early on, I am not thinking about musical skills.

Grow into the Shoes

God gifted me with musical abilities adequate for music leading early on. I had early experience with singing and instrumental training and music theory before I graduated high school. Do I wish I'd have had help with guitar earlier? Definitely. Would I have benefitted from technical help about sound systems in those early days? Certainly. Do I wish I could have led worship in a modern band back then? Yeah, that would have been cool.

But when I think back about my mentoring gap, I am not thinking about those things much. I wish someone would have challenged me to think about the lyric content of our songs, to consider whether they were biblically faithful. I wish someone would have challenged me to think critically about standing before our people in a pastoral role (not necessarily *office,* but role) rather than primarily a musical one. I wish someone would have been alongside me helping me focus on the *substance* of our worship over the *experience* of it, someone spurring me to love our Savior and loving his people over loving the music. These things aren't mutually exclusive – as though I must choose to either love the Savior or the music – but they *are* ordered – some deserve priority while others have secondary importance. By God's grace I have for many years been growing into these shoes he has set before me, and lately, I hope, more than ever. Still, I have no doubt I would have grown sooner and faster had I gone after it aggressively early on, especially through formal theological training and mentoring.

I want you to grow into the gospel shoes he has set before you in your own context. I am convinced that if you will start NOW to aggressively pursue growth, God will work in and through you in ways you will not be able to imagine.

Chapter 4: Kneel in the Shoes

As you take the stage clad in your influence – your "skinny jeans" – I have challenged you to look carefully at the responsibility into which God is calling you to step – into your "fat shoes." I have pointed out that these shoes carry the name and reputation of Jesus himself, that these are branded by his gospel. I have warned you of the consequence of leading God's people laced up in knock-offs and urged you instead to take the stage only in true gospel shoes so you sing life to your people and help them teach each other these words of life. I have charged you to actively and aggressively seek to grow into these true gospel shoes, for your own sake and for the sake of those whom you lead. This growing is a lifelong, even eternal, process for all of us. *See* the shoes, *step into* the shoes and *grow* into the shoes. Now I want to charge you to *kneel* in the shoes.

Here I want to address the underlying *mindset* for wearing the shoes, and then give practical counsel for how to express that mindset in your worship-leading activities. Jesus gave us a *picture* of this mindset when he washed his disciples' feet, as recorded in John 13. He commanded them, "So if I, your Lord and Teacher, have washed your feet, you also ought to wash one another's feet. For I have given you an example, that you also should do just as I have done for you" (vv.14-15).

If Jesus gave us a picture, Paul gave us an *explanation*: "Adopt the same attitude as that of Christ Jesus..." (Philippians 2:5). What is that attitude? Paul goes on to explain the unimaginable way that Jesus, God himself, humbled himself to serve God the Father and serve mankind to the point of death on a cross. Jesus' attitude of humble servitude was announced ahead of time by the prophet Isaiah, who described the Messiah as a suffering servant, especially in Isaiah 52-53. Isaiah's description was fulfilled perfectly and completely by Jesus in his crucifixion.

Since we are not likely to be crucified, the foot-washing picture is super helpful. When you take the stage, you take the position of Jesus in this picture. You are likely one of the best musicians in your church. If you have pursued growth as suggested in the last chapter, you may well be better biblically informed than most in your church. By nature of your role, and possibly even more so because of personal charisma, you likely have more influence than almost anyone else in your congregation. With all that, your calling is to follow Jesus. He got down on the dirty floor and did the dirty work of a servant. That's what you and I are supposed to do too.

Jesus did not empty himself of his deity (though that is a common misunderstanding of Philippians 2) or act as though he was *not* the greatest teacher or as if he were unable to heal or control the weather. He didn't give up his *identity*. He gave up his *rights*. That's what you and I are to do. You take every good gift God has given you – a beautiful voice, killer instrumental chops, magnetic personality, whatever it is – and when you walk up on the stage you get down on your knees to serve. Kneel in the shoes.

Aside from the biblical descriptions and pictures of humble servant leadership, I have seen examples of kneeling in the shoes in my own experiences. I mentioned before that I did not come up in ministry under any formal mentorships. I would, however, say that I did have some mentors, though they might be unaware – or even surprised – to find out I see them that way. There are a number of people who lived out gospel ministry before me in such a way that I knew I should emulate what I saw in them. One of those people stands out in my mind as a church leader who served in humility like his Master. His name was Ron Baker.

"Brother Baker," as everyone called him, was dynamite bundled in a little package, filled with energy and little hints of feistiness. He was a classy dude, and full of style. When I met him, he was better than twice my age, nearing his seventies, but you would never believe that based on his pace. He even played some pick-up basketball at the park with some of us church people once, and you could still see flashes of the b-ball legend I learned he was back in his prime. What made that even more remarkable was that he was one of the few grown men I've ever been able to look down on physically. I'm about 5' 8" and I had him by maybe six inches.

But in every other way, all I ever did was look *up* to Ron Baker. When we moved our family from Denver to a smallish Kansas town, God led us to a long-established Baptist church where Ron had led the music as a volunteer for well over thirty years. Out of loving service, he did the hard work putting together and leading the music for his mid-size congregation. This was IN ADDITION to working as a small business owner for nearly all those years, as Ron and his twin brother owned shoe shops (so appropriate now that I think of it). So, he worked long hours every week managing shoe repair and purchasing and sales before ever putting on his *gospel* shoes for his church. I know he had his faults like any of us, but this diminutive man that I came to know and quickly came to love was a giant. Here is why I consider him a mentor and hero, and here is why I commend him to you now as an example. Ron Baker was a servant who led with confidence balanced with humility. He knew how to kneel down in his gospel shoes and to serve like his Savior.

This is why I consider Brother Baker my mentor. He volunteered for nearly 40 years before he was finally honored with a part-time staff position, but he had as much to do with the shaping of that church as any full-time senior pastor. He prepared each week, selecting songs and then pulling out sheet music and putting it into folders for all the musicians. He was ready to go for rehearsals, and ready to direct, but also open to ideas and suggestions. He brought energy to a traditional musical scene for decades – piano, organ, choir and some brass doing classic selections from mostly the 19th to early 20th century – but he was aware of the new trends in church music. By the time we came to the church Ron had been introducing contemporary songs into the church repertoire. He was not afraid of change, he liked much of the new stuff, and he seemed convinced it would serve the church well, probably even better, in the coming generation.

Ron was aware of himself, his own capacities and limitations. His willingness to place the church's needs over his own position and status was what earned my respect over most anything else. At one point, he was having problems with his throat that really hampered his freedom in singing. As the trouble persisted, he asked me if I would be willing to take over fronting the worship. At the time, I was playing and singing in the band (some bass, some drums and sometimes keys) as well as singing in the choir. At his request, I happily began to lead the singing, and he seemed very happy to play his trumpet in the horn section. This situation persisted for a few weeks.

Then one day Ron approached me again. His voice was fine now, but he wasn't suggesting a return to the status quo. He explained that while he loved the new music, it was difficult for him to lead it well. He felt I was more effective at leading the congregation and directing the band in these musical settings that were more native to me. He was enjoying playing his horn and wondered if I'd be willing to continue to serve essentially as the worship leader while he stayed in the brass section.

I was blown away. Ron showed a real servant attitude. He wanted what he believed was best for the church. He had concluded that it was time for the hand-off. He had led the congregation in singing the gospel to and with one another for decades, but he knew someone else would carry them on in the coming years and generations. The humility he showed in that transition was inspiring.

Make no mistake. Ron Baker was confident, tireless, dedicated, and a bit fiery, but he was a servant. And he was joyful. I could tell that all those years of serving well had given him joy. It showed up in the songs he wrote. To this day, Ron is the only one with whom I have ever significantly collaborated on songwriting, and even there he showed his humility. I remember his asking for me to bring some contemporary perspective on helping him finish out chords and structures to go with his lyrics and melodies for a few songs – what a privilege! I was struck that while I – who was in my thirties – tended to write ballads, Ron seemed to write mostly peppy praise songs!

It's probably very evident the affinity I have for Ron. I have good reasons to remember him so fondly. The attitude I remember seeing in him is the same one I commend to you. Be a servant leader in your congregation. Like Ron Baker, model your ministry after Christ. Take your gifts and your energy and serve.

First, serve the Master who gave you your gifts. If Christ, who is God himself, was willing to set aside his rightful status to humbly serve the will of the Father to the point of death – even death by crucifixion – then certainly we who are made in his image ought to do the same. Jesus didn't merely wash his disciples' feet (John 13:1-11), but he also explained to them that by doing so he was setting a pattern for their own humble service (v.15). Serve Christ in your jeans and shoes. Take his priorities for your own. Seek to reveal and honor him before your people, to make him known to them that they may love him as you do. Serve him with energy, with diligence and patience. Serve him in the mundane things, like rehearsing when you'd rather not, or listening to yet another one of that band member's seemingly endless suggestions. Seek him in prayer to learn what he wants from your Sunday set list, your Thursday prep and even your Friday night hangout with your friends.

Second, serve your congregation. Don't make too much of the criticisms OR the pats on the back. Work hard at figuring out what will best help them rehearse the gospel together. Find the balance between what they want and what they need. Set the table the best you can for them, and then invite them to feast. When it comes to music, there are a few key areas to effectively address, and I will do so in some practical detail later on. Most important, as I've already mentioned, is to choose songs full of gospel richness and faithfulness. Then remove as many obstacles and distractions as you can. This means you have to come to know your congregation, to know what will likely overwhelm them.

The practical list goes on and on, and you will keep tweaking your own criteria as you grow, but the fundamental issue is to think like a servant. With your primary focus on serving Christ well, set a secondary focus on serving your people well as a means to fulfill that primary obligation to Christ. I have learned over the years that many people discern a worship leader that is serving them from one that is serving himself or herself. Be the first kind of worship leader.

Then, as you serve Christ and his people, your next priority is your fellow musicians. How can you build them up, challenge them, even help them grow spiritually and musically? Serving your teammates might mean giving them more freedom or input into how to approach the songs. On the other hand, it might mean helping them realize the times they need to dial it back and make space for their bandmates. You might need to encourage a player or singer who is self-conscious. You might need to have a tough conversation with someone who is trying to operate outside their skillset and inadvertently sabotaging the band's effectiveness. It's impossible to list all the ways you'll need to serve your fellow musicians, but once again the attitude of humble service is the engine that must drive you as a leader. Like your congregants, your music team members can probably tell when you are loving them well by your servant attitude.

When you order your priorities this way as a servant – when you kneel in your gospel shoes – you'll generally find that you will enjoy your own blessings as a result. As you serve Christ, his people, and your fellow musicians, you can expect to experience the true joy of ministry like my brother Ron Baker did for so long, and like I have for many years myself. Regardless how any particular Sunday comes off, if you have set out to faithfully serve in your gospel shoes you can at least be certain of the joy that is before you when you meet Christ face to face. Just as Jesus set our pattern for service, he sets our pattern for joy, as the writer of Hebrews makes clear: "Let us run with endurance the race that lies before us, keeping our eyes on Jesus, the pioneer and perfecter of our faith. For the joy that lay before him, he endured the cross, despising the shame, and sat down at the right hand of God" (Hebrews 12:1b-2). Aim for that joy by following Jesus in humble service.

Chapter 5: Stand in the Shoes

We'll draw more from that race analogy in Hebrews in the next chapter, but first I need to discuss the static reality that defines not only your starting line but also your progress all the way to the finish. The gospel sets your course. As you discover and celebrate the true gospel, you discover who you are in Christ, both as an individual and as a minister. The gospel's identity and yours are linked. If you begin to veer away from the true gospel, you will be veering off course in your race, and as you do, you will begin to see a deceptive and empty version of yourself. So, in this metaphor mash-up, odd as it sounds, I will urge you to *stand* in the shoes as you *run* in them. It's okay. Both terms are figurative, so you won't trip up trying to do both at the same time. In fact, following the biblical principles will *keep* you from tripping. So, first let me talk about standing.

The true gospel keeps your eyes fixed on Jesus, and when that happens God may enable you to do amazing things, like Peter's water-walk. But, like with Peter, if you let your gaze drift elsewhere, you will find yourself drowning in chaos. You and I need a bedrock that is unchanging as we go through a stormy sea of opinions and preferences, not only for our ministries' sakes but for our own. That bedrock is, of course, the true gospel. We must stand in our gospel shoes, and that is not a one-time, momentary decision but rather must be the ongoing, daily, even moment-by-moment reality of our lives and ministries.

The basis of the bedrock metaphor comes from Jesus himself, from his words in Matthew 7:

> *"Therefore, everyone who hears these words of mine and acts on them will be like a wise man who built his house on the rock. The rain fell, the rivers rose, and the winds blew and pounded that house. Yet it didn't collapse, because its foundation was on the rock. But everyone who hears these words of mine and doesn't act on them*

will be like a foolish man who built his house on the sand. The rain fell, the rivers rose, the winds blew and pounded that house, and it collapsed. It collapsed with a great crash."

We understand "these words of mine" to summarily refer to the true gospel. If we order our lives according to that, we are building like the wise man. If we reject that gospel and build our lives - and our ministries - on any other foundation, we know what to expect. Perhaps you can still hear the onomatopoeia from the old kids' song in your ears: "splat!"

There are a lot of sandy foundations available for your worship leading ministry. If you are like me, you are offered a good many on a weekly basis, probably a handful of them on Sunday mornings alone!

The music is too loud.
Why doesn't the choir sing more?
Ebenezer – really?
The band should wear nicer clothes.
Turn up the subs.
Do we really have to repeat the bridge that many times?
We don't sing enough hymns.
Why do we sing ABOUT God so much but not TO him?
Do you realize where your bass player was last night?
Why are the songs always so slow?
I like your haircut.
Could the singer cover her tattoos?

Of course, for any sample I offer there are complete opposite opinions. If we are not careful, the congregation we serve may compel us to build a ministry founded on sand. So too may our creative community. Or our heroes. Or our fellow leaders, possibly even including pastors. We are all susceptible to sandy foundations. Remember, this is in fact why we gather to worship. We must remind ourselves of what the gospel really is, so we can reorient our opinions and conversations from that perspective.

Every issue represented above – and thousands more – may have some validity in conversations about our worship gatherings, but they are periphery. They only matter as it relates to the degree to which they enhance or impede the church's ability to faithfully obey the New Testament commands regarding corporate worship. How do these things help or hinder as we gather in gospel-centered worship of the one true God, known through his Son, Jesus Christ? If you build your ministry identity on any particular popular cultural collective, you may feel good about your program for a few months or maybe even years, but the sands will shift. Storms will come. They have a purging effect. Everything that is not bedrock gets swept away. When that happens, the ministry struggles with its identity. Usually, so does the minister.

Make no mistake. The storms come even when you *are* standing on bedrock. But you are not swept away. If you have built your ministry on the bedrock, then that is not swept away either. Whatever is lost is cosmetic – it may be reassessed in rebuilding, but the bones are sound. That's what I want for you. The security of a personal identity and a ministry identity that are both anchored in bedrock. I want you to stand in your gospel shoes.

The Apostle Paul used the term "stand" in this way a lot, especially as a challenging call to "stand firm." Let me highlight. He closed his first letter to the Corinthian church this way. After much rebuke over divisions and ungodly pagan behaviors, and after laying out for them what worship should look like, he wrote, "Be alert, **stand firm** in the faith, be courageous, be strong. Do everything in love." Apparently, his challenge was answered. For in a later letter he said, "… for we are workers with you for your joy, because you **stand firm** in your faith." (Note the mention of joy once again with gospel-centeredness.) On the other hand, when the Galatian church was being pulled toward the other extreme opposite paganism – Jewish legalism – he used the same term to pull the Galatians to the same gospel center: "For freedom, Christ set us free. **Stand firm**, then, and don't submit again to a yoke of slavery."

It was very clear from his writings that Paul's great desire for the churches was gospel fidelity. He exposed his own emotional connection to the prospect of their faithfulness when writing in 1 Thessalonians 3:8, "…we were encouraged about you through your faith. For now we live, if you **stand firm** in the Lord." In his second letter to these believers, Paul reiterated the reality of God's call to them through the gospel he and others had delivered. He then said, "So then, brothers and sisters, **stand firm** and hold to the traditions you were taught…" These were apostolic traditions summarizing the true gospel, things that are essential to salvation, not the traditional trappings of worship preferences.

Another great early church apostle, Peter, spoke much the same way. He wrote his first letter addressing the theme of Christian suffering, mostly from the outside by satanic opposition. After a brief section addressing church leaders in particular – the elders – he neared the conclusion of his letter saying, "I have written to you briefly in order to encourage you and to testify that this is the true grace of God. **Stand firm** in it." The context of the letter, and the immediate context of the previous verse, shows this "true grace" as the content of the gospel. This grace allows us to stand firm through suffering. That suffering does not always come from *outside* the church. Many times, our foundations are also challenged from *within* the church.

What does this challenge to stand firm mean practically in your ministry work? It means you must work hard at maintaining the aspects of corporate worship that do not change. Stand firm in biblical truth regardless of what forms the expressions take.

The New Testament gives us a lot of freedom about the periphery. *Should this song be led from acoustic guitar only rather than the whole band? Should we have a choir next week? What key is best? Should we sing while collecting the offering? Could we teach through a panel discussion some time? Do we provide robes, or just baptize people in their street clothes?*

All the above questions ask about periphery but hidden within them are issues of the core. The New Testament church is commanded to sing. We have many options to consider when trying to determine how best to do that, but at the end of the day we should be committed to be a singing church. We have a lot of ways to encourage Christians to live out God's pattern of generosity, but whatever approach we take, we must be committed to be a giving church. There are many ways to expose and reflect upon what the Bible says, but we must commit to be a Bible teaching church. We can hand out robes or not, build a tank in our buildings or go to a river or lake. We can practice open or closed communion, passing out the elements or forming lines to dip the bread, but we must be a church committed to observing the ordinances commanded by Christ. These things must be foundational for your ministry.

What does the call to stand mean for you personally? Find your identity in the gospel, not in celebrity. Not in musical prowess nor the lack thereof (yes, I've seen people boast in their inabilities). Not in charisma nor the lack of it. Not in your fashion sense nor your cool factor. Not in a cultural tradition, nor a cutting-edge trend. You should not even find your identity ultimately in the opinions of leadership partners or mentors, though they should be the first among those that help you stay centered in the proper identity. Your identity should be found only in Christ and his gospel. Why do I press this point?

Perhaps most appropriate for our purposes here is a charge that brings us back to Paul. He gives a reminder to his pastoral protégé, Timothy, in 2 Timothy 2:19: "Nevertheless, God's solid foundation **stands firm**, bearing this inscription: The Lord knows who are his, and let everyone who calls on the name of the Lord turn away from wickedness." In this case, Paul has already issued his challenge for Timothy to ignore the periphery and stay focused on the gospel, what in verse 15 he calls "the word of truth." He names some who have "departed" from this truth and then points Timothy to his bedrock, God's solid foundation.

Notice how tightly identity is tied to the gospel. In fact, Paul's Old Testament reference, "The Lord knows who are his," points back to a sort of worship leader challenge way back during the journey between the exodus from Egypt and on the way to the promised land of Canaan. A guy named Korah rounded up some likeminded malcontents against Moses (pretty much the lead pastor/worship leader of Israel in the wilderness, along with his brother Aaron). Korah essentially asked, "What makes YOU so special that we have to do it your way?" Moses responded, "The Lord will reveal who he chooses to come near him."

Moses' opinions didn't inherently matter anymore than Korah's or anyone else's. Nor do yours or mine. The issue was that Moses was appointed by God to lead, and that his leadership was oriented around God's own word. Korah quickly turned "the whole community" against Moses and Aaron. God was ready to take them ALL out, had Moses not appealed for mercy on their behalf. Still, Korah and his whole bunch were swallowed alive by the ground, and they "vanished from the assembly."

Sooner or later, a Korah will make a stir in YOUR assembly. They will challenge your leadership, demanding to know what makes your opinions more important than theirs. The answer is, "Nothing." If you stake your leadership choices on your opinions alone, you have nothing on which to stand firm. But if instead your ministry is built on the gospel, if your decisions are oriented around what helps your assembly focus on and rehearse and live out that gospel, then you can stand firm.

When this is true, your heart will break for your Korah, but his challenge will not break you. You will be able to honestly consider his opinions, to weigh them against what is core and stand firm in your assessments. You may realize some changes are in order, or you may be affirmed that your current practices truly are the best option for the moment. What you will *not* do is lose *your* identity or your *ministry's* identity in the periphery. You stand firm in the gospel, and everything else you hold loosely. At the end of the day, the Lord knows who are his, and he has given you the influence of leadership. If you first find your foundation in the gospel, then you can make the best decisions about what best serves your God and your people, knowing and resting on that bedrock.

Of course, it is true that you should invite other perspectives and regularly re-evaluate best practices for your ministry. That will be the focus of the next chapter. As you do, you will still have some – perhaps many – who will refuse to be satisfied with your choices. You will grieve over some who leave your congregation. You will likely grieve worse over some who refuse to leave but also refuse to stop complaining! What will that do to you? How will you respond?

Stand in the shoes. Keep yourself founded on the true gospel. Build your ministry on and around that. The naysayers will perplex you and grieve you, but you will remember your foundation and your calling. Stand firm. Keep loving them and pointing them back to center. Let all those difficult conversations be about recognizing true worship from idolatry – core from periphery – rather than about vanilla and chocolate – mere preferences.

The Korahs of your ministry are not your only danger, perhaps not even your worst danger. Public opinion is a sandy foundation. That is not only true when the storms of malcontents hit. It is also true on those calm, peaceful, fair-weather Sundays when the beach is quiet, and you have deluded yourself into thinking God is happy with your church's worship just because everyone else seems to be happy with it. If your foundation is not the bedrock of the true gospel, you will eventually lose your footing in your knockoff shoes and slip into the chaotic sea. Or perhaps you will sit comfortably for a good long while in your beach house, but you will still have the unsettling, empty feeling that comes from a shifting foundation –

not too sure of anything but sort of surfing the fleeting pleasure of the moment.

That's dangerous for you, and it's dangerous for the people in front of you. Instead, keep your eyes on the prize. Keep digging deeper into the true gospel. Keep growing in it. Commit yourself to serving in it. Stand in it. All the way to the end. When come the Korahs, stand only in the gospel. When come the pats on the back, stand only in the gospel. When culture shifts, stand in the timeless eternal gospel – the same one Paul and Peter stood in. Keep your shoes firmly fixed on this unchanging reality as the foundation for your own identity and that of the ministry to which God has called you.

Chapter 6: Run in the Shoes

In the last chapter I focused on the theological grounding of your worship leader identity, the unchanging gospel reality in which you stand as you move through life. In this chapter I will talk about the need for practical adaptability – the shaping and reshaping of the *expressions* of that reality. The way we in our church have expressed this need is this: reflection and innovation.

Reflection helps us ensure we are keeping the true gospel pure in our ministry while innovation helps us figure out how to ensure that the true gospel is finding effective expression in our current forms and practices. Think of the old missionary analogy: we must guard the content while adapting the container. We must preserve the true gospel, but we must also innovate in allowable ways that express that gospel in meaningful ways relative to our time and situation.

The picture painted in Hebrews 12:1-2 is of a runner poised in a snapshot moment before a marathon. The call is to set aside everything that would hinder the runner, and then to run with endurance. I have urged you to set aside false gospels and trivial or selfish motives as you lace up your running shoes. I have urged you to have the same particular finish line in focus as does the runner in Hebrews – namely, Jesus. There is (by God's grace) a long course ahead between here and there. This course is defined by the true gospel. You either stay on course or you veer away from it.

Now let me tweak the picture. Marathons are usually run on paved streets, but this long race is more like a cross-country one. Staying on course is really important because you don't want to get your people lost in the trees or the wilderness. But even as you stay on course, you will be running on a variety of terrains. Different segments of your race will require different strategies, even different gear. In this race you do not have the opportunity to run the course ahead of time. You may have some pretty good guesses about what is ahead, but when it comes to it, you will need to assess on the fly.

Thankfully, God has not only set your course according to his Word, but he has also given you a Counselor and Guide to help you discern how best to adjust when your setting takes a turn. Running in the shoes means you will have to constantly seek the Holy Spirit's direction in prayer, asking for wisdom. There are many good resources to help you grow in the crucial discipline of prayer, and I encourage you to draw from them to discover the biblical principles that drive effective prayer. Suffice it here to say that you must remain desperate to discover, understand and align yourself with God's agenda for your worship-leading ministry.

Broadly, that agenda is clear: exalt God through his Son, Christ, in Spirit-led worship guarded by the truth of the gospel. However, the possible expressions of obedience to that agenda are as diverse as God has made his creatures who carry it out. You must lean hard on the Spirit to help you understand the best way to help your congregation be faithful worshipers in any given season or even a given moment.

Sometimes in your race you settle into a good groove, confident you are faithfully on the gospel path. Then the course bends a new direction. Remember, the way I am using the analogy this is not a shift in gospel *truth* but rather a shift in gospel *expression*, a change in your *context*. The gospel hasn't changed but your environment has. There has been a shift in your culture or demographics. The course probably had begun to shift a while ago, but you hadn't noticed. Now you realize that it seems to be *over there* while you (and your congregation) are still cruising along *over here*. To follow the true gospel path into this new context means a shift, and you notice it will carry you into a steep climb, no less.

You will be tempted to keep going straight ahead with the familiar and comfortable and easy route. Don't do it. The shift you see is a subtle shift from letting the gospel define your direction to letting status quo define it. Trappings and periphery (fine in and of themselves) are dangerously close to becoming idols. If this happens, you've left your sure footing and you will stumble. So will a lot of the people following you.

Many churches have made this mistake over and over again. One generation of a local congregation organically settles into a pattern of gospel expressions in their worship, as they should. But then months and years pass. The broader community around them changes in various ways, but the church keeps doing what is comfortable for themselves. Eventually, visitors come and go because the culture of this church – its gospel expressions – are foreign to them. Gradually, what happens is the congregation grows older and smaller and less diverse together.

There are two horrible problems exposed in this far too common storyline. The first is Kingdom retraction verses Kingdom expansion. The church becomes focused on herself rather than on the lost. When she does this, she *herself* gets lost, much like Bilbo and the dwarves when they got off the path through Mirkwood. The second problem I mentioned already. True worship has become idolatry. When you wander from the gospel, you will get disoriented and the giant spiders of consumerism will bind you and suck you dry! (If you don't know what I'm talking about, please go right out and read The Hobbit, or at least stream the movie.)

On what basis do I make these claims? Watch any church revitalization project. See new leaders challenge the charter members to reach out in evangelism, to welcome seekers and newer Christians into the congregation. Hear them urge the old guard to make contextual accommodations – not doctrinal ones, mind you, but ones of expression – to provide an environment more native to the current community and culture. The beast of idolatry will show itself. Members will question, resist and complain about the suggestions. Power centers will emerge as representatives rise up against the "dangerous" new ideas. In every case, stress. In many cases outright war. You've heard of worship wars? I've been in a few. I've seen people leaving a church or trying to kick out a pastor because a piece of furniture got moved.

How does this happen? It happens when we as leaders fail to keep reflection and innovation as a regular habit. When the gospel path shifts into a new context, we cannot afford to let ourselves or our people begin to confuse the contents with the container. Doing things the way we have done them for years may be comfortable, but we must not find our comfort in a certain look to a room, a certain musical style or instrumentation, a certain order of service. Our comfort must be found in the true gospel, in our Savior alone. Just as we must stand firm in the nonnegotiable content of the gospel, we must *refuse* to stand firm in the widely negotiable expressions of that gospel. "Guard the deposit," says Paul. I would add this: Don't argue over the design of the checkbook cover.

Take a lesson from whatever version of worship war you might see. The problem isn't that new wave is better than old school and the old-schoolers need to realize it. The problem is that we are confused about where to stand firm and what to hold loosely. You do the church no favors if you fight the good fight to expose all the idols of the old-school generation only to replace their idols with your own. At some point you will be where they are, confronted by a shift in the context. A faithful gospel ministry will require some tweaks on your part.

When that happens, don't cling to what is comfortable. Instead, take on the new terrain and innovate as needed. Help your brothers and sisters understand the need and adapt too. Easier said than done, but that is your calling. Remember, your sure footing is only on the gospel course laid out before you. You must stay the course. That does not mean the course won't take you into new and unexpected realities. Eventually, you will have to do gospel ministry in new contexts that will require tweaks in your approach. I mentioned that my mentor Ron Baker realized this, and he went with the shift that was needed. You'll need to do the same.

150 years ago, it was as normal as the day is long to ride downtown in Kansas City on a horse. Today that would be weird and dangerous and quite possibly illegal. 100 years ago, if you wanted to communicate quickly

to the masses, you'd have to go to the newspaper office or a radio station. Today, you'd better get something to go viral on social media. 20 years ago, there were some stretches of road in the United States, where you had better hope your car didn't break down because you might be stranded for days before someone passed by. Now, the only concern is whether you can get a signal on your cell phone.

Ministry contexts are changing more rapidly than ever, and there are a huge variety of contexts even without the advance of technology. For years my sister and her family ministered in a town of only a couple thousand in western Kansas where the "worship team" consisted of exactly the members of their family. The only tech was a microphone and a piano. By contrast, for more than two months of this year our current church in Kansas City was able to "meet" only in a virtual sense. That was all done through streaming software, music and video editing software, mobile phones, laptops, and the high-speed internet at my home.

If you want a powerful example of the kinds of shifts that demand ministry innovation, I need only to mention this: Covid-19. When the whole world shut down in early 2020, churches everywhere were forced rapid-fire into a scramble to figure out how to be the church without being able to actually meet in person (only for a while, we hoped). This less-than-ideal situation was forcing us to figure out how to make the most of our gospel ministry in a radically different paradigm. At this writing, we are still wrestling with whether or how it is worth it to try to obey our command to sing the gospel together in assembly when we are being required to wear masks over our mouths and noses.

Thankfully, this situation is extremely unique. Still, innovation is always a given necessity for effective church ministry. It is especially important as it relates to the handing off of the gospel deposit from one generation to the next. This is the struggle of ministers in the host of revitalization projects going on in the many congregations that have been in decline for years. Oh, and Church Planter, do not think you are off the hook for long, either. For the culture that feels native and natural to your young congregation now will feel old school much sooner than you might think!

For many months now, we have been trying to refocus and rejuvenate a 75-year-old congregation. Before that, the other current staff pastor and I worked together at a church he helped plant fewer than 25 years ago. That church already feels very different from what it was even five years ago. What is important is that the gospel foundation is the same, even while we try to reimagine how it is best expressed in our current setting.

As you run your gospel course as a servant leader, you will need to adapt along the way. This means you'll need to know and remember what is core and essential, so you not only stay focused on that but also discern what may be adapted to your context and what may not. In our race metaphor imagine the gospel not only as the course that directs you but also as the sponsor whom you advertise all over your running suit. You may have different gear appropriate for different legs of the race, but every iteration of your gear displays that true gospel brand, just like the shoes.

Having laid the above groundwork, let me offer some practical advice from principles that have emerged from my own experiences. I have led congregational worship in a wide variety of settings from small church to big church, traditional to contemporary, solo on a guitar or piano to directing a full orchestra or modern rock band. So, let me walk through some considerations with which you are likely to need to wrestle.

Adapt your musical forms to deliver gospel truth as effectively as possible. A lead pastor once asked me if I thought there were "right" musical styles for congregational worship. My response was – and is – that I think there are styles that are more or less accommodating or effective for that setting. I can imagine a diverse group of people catching on to and singing together with worship songs delivered through most music forms, but it seems like there are some exceptions.

Run in the Shoes

There was a time when a long melisma (singing one syllable over many pitch movements) was a typical element of vocal music in a church setting (think Handel's Messiah). However, even when it was common, I'm not sure it was easy for a typical congregant to participate. Certainly, for most people today the Baroque style that employs that technique would alienate many from singing along in corporate worship.

On the flip side, as I've observed rap music rising in popularity I've wondered if that would serve congregations well in their singing together. So far, I've concluded that some might well be useful, but that the rapid-fire lyrics that set many rappers apart might again be beyond the ability of many churchgoers. More than that, it would be hard to synchronize together in a coherent gospel proclamation.

So, while I like both forms and I'm open to either in the church setting, I'm guessing Baroque and rap will have some challenges to overcome. Maybe those challenges will be met. Who knows? Many styles are more easily suited to group sing-along, but I think few if any styles are *inherently* inappropriate for corporate worship but only may be *practically* so in some cases.

It is typical to settle into a normal range of musical styles that fit your church context. Many churches seek variety in multiple services while others commit to blending within a given service. Of course, there will undoubtedly be some variety in any setting, and I think that is a value to pursue. A narrow range may be comfortable for those who enjoy that range, but it can also numb those same people while alienating others. A decent range of styles seems to be the wise option, so long as they are used in ways that are accessible to the average non-musician.

Similarly, you want to serve the crowd well in terms of grooves and energy. Anyone planning a concert or show knows you must mix up slow songs with faster ones, contemplative ballads with high-energy celebration. The worship planner does the same, though her highest goal isn't the satisfaction of the attendee but rather the ability of that person to stay engaged in worship. God is creative, and he has made us in his image. So, we are creative in our worship planning. We include variety because he does. We rehearse the gospel in different musical settings because its many themes are expressed in a variety of ways. A song lyric focused on victory or everlasting life is inappropriately set in a funeral dirge. A song of confession and lament should not likely have a tempo marking of 144 bpm. You are most likely a creative, and these ideas are in your wheelhouse.

What you may not always remember is to not leave the non-creatives you serve in the dust. I'll put it this way: aim for singability. The idea of singability is really the broad concept driving everything practical I've been suggesting so far. It's hard for many people to sing in "legit" musical styles like Baroque. It's hard for many to keep up with complex vocal syncopations. It gets difficult for most people to stay engaged for three straight ballads that are acoustic-driven with the same keyboard pad sound underneath, all paced between 72 and 80 bpm. So, yeah, mix it up a little. *You* know that something different musically is happening on each of those four repeats of the bridge, but that musical development may just feel like a lot of the same thing to *them*. Remember to serve your congregation.

I don't know how many years I have bounced here and there on the question of song keys. Some would say keep the pitch range within a certain limit, say, an octave and a half. Others would say, set your keys where they are best suited for your band and or vocalists and let the crowd figure it out. It is true that most people who listen to their favorites in the car or at home or wherever will follow along with recording artists going way outside their own ranges and figure out how to adjust. Still, people tend to be less bold when singing in church, at least if they're not in a setting where the worship band drowns out everyone not on stage. (That, by the way, is *not* a normative pattern for fulfilling the New Testament mandate to help the church sing *together*.) Even if you decide a limited pitch range is a good idea, you have to decide where it should be centered.

Do I keep most dudes and the altos happy, or do I accommodate tenors and let the ladies join them in the same octave? How about the popular octave jump that helps the song build intensity? If they can't make the jump, they just stay down, right?

Well, over the years of deliberation, I've fallen into a fairly eclectic position. There is wisdom in all the perspectives I've sampled here, and more besides, but the best advice I can offer is to avoid extremes as norms. It's probably okay to do that 8va to rebuild the bridge after the breakdown chorus, but I wouldn't do that on three songs of your four-song set. It's probably good to have one song in the alto-friendly key for your female lead vocal and for another song to be in that range that might force the basses to drop down on the high chorus. They *will* figure it out. One tool that helps your congregants make these adjustments turns out to be a great help in a lot of ways: familiarity.

I've heard a worship leader say nothing affects crowd participation as much as familiarity. They're probably right. The congregation's familiarity with a song may allow you to push the envelope on a number of things: complexity, challenging rhythms, breakdowns or a cappella moments, or maybe even raps! If your crowd knows a song really well – like eyes-closed well – you can mark it down that they will sing louder and better and be generally more engaged than with an unfamiliar or new song. If they stumbled over some tricky parts when you first introduced it, they'll probably do just fine once they know that song inside and out. What you have to decide is whether that song has enough gospel payoff to make it a classic for your people. If you conclude that it does, then go for it. They'll get there, probably even if they didn't really like the song at first.

I related earlier in this book how regular and repeated exposure to a few 80's songs caused me to come to enjoy them (musically, at least) even though I was initially trained to reject them on basis of both style and substance. When I hear those songs, there is just a comforting nostalgia that comes over me. (Remember, that's why you have to be careful about the content of those songs you are teaching your people to love.) This will happen in church too. Access that as a tool. Select really good gospel songs to burn into the souls of your congregants. If they are a little bit challenging musically, that will be overcome over time.

Still, while familiarity helps you access some more difficult or complex songs, I think as a rule it is wise to build the bulk of your repertoire on songs that are fairly easy to pick up on quickly. One way to explore creativity in balance with ease of singability is to reserve the complexity for the instrumentation. You can do really cool stuff with the band while still keeping the songs easy to sing. Of course, remember that you must serve your bandmates too. Don't overwhelm them but try to find ways to let them express their chops for God's glory as they worship too. (Remember to help them learn discernment about showing off those chops. You don't want the FOH engineer to have to turn down your lead guitarist for playing a glam rock solo over "Just As I Am." Been there, done that.)

Another contextualization you should think about on a regular basis is instrumentation. There are many options available in our world today. The good old piano and organ are still around, as are classical instruments found in symphonic orchestras. Throw in modern electronic instruments and the innovations of the digital age that make sequencing and ambient loops available for little or no money, and you have quite a palette with which to work. Which combinations of these are available to you? Which resonate with the current culture of your church body? What capacities do you have to coordinate, direct or even instruct potential musicians? You'll need to think through these options as you run in your gospel shoes. You'll probably have a norm that is your current staple, but you'll want to mix it up. It may well get mixed up *for* you as musicians come and go, as your church cycles in size, and as the culture of the congregation shifts.

One category of diversity you should consider comes right out of Scripture. Paul talks in a couple of his letters about the songs the church should sing together. In both places (Ephesians 5:19 and Colossians 3:16) he specifically mentions "psalms, hymns, and spiritual songs." We generally take these categories to encompass all kinds of songs that glorify God and are appropriate for group singing. Of course, the psalms are a specific category found in the Old Testament itself. And we find hymns and spiritual songs written not only in the Scriptures but by a host of the saints over the last two millennia – some of them perhaps by you!

I would encourage you to treat your song sets like a healthy meal. Include the whole range from hardy meats to vital veggies and even dessert. Make sure your set list has some deep, gospel-rich songs. Especially helpful are songs that replay the gospel story of Christ's death for sins, burial, and resurrection according to the Scriptures. It is good to sing songs both *about* God and *to* God. Find a good balance between mind and heart. Balance songs loaded with multiple verses of robust biblical lyrics with songs of fewer lyrics that allow space for meditation on and adoration of Christ, his intrinsic beauty and his amazing work. A good worship set follows the spirit-and-truth criteria, helping us worship with mind and heart, our whole selves.

Evaluate songs by their content. As with biblical interpretation, you will find it wise to consider the writers' broader bodies of work to guard the way your own congregation will understand the lyrics they are singing. If a song has ambiguous language that is likely to theologically trip up your people, find another song that is clearer. Or at minimum, take a moment to explain how that song should be faithfully understood before singing it. There are thousands of biblically solid and clear and compelling songs to put on the lips and in the hearts of your people. Don't settle for less.

In addition to all the above issues related to music, you may need to innovate in other practical ways. It wasn't long ago that most churches still sang out of hymnals but now lyrics projected on screens are far more common. Churches used to be built with architecture that focused on a central pulpit, choir area and baptistry. Now many church buildings are multi-purpose structures designed with theatrical lighting and concert venue sound systems.

You should be thinking through how these things impact the effectiveness of gospel-centered worship in your congregation. For example, I visited a church that had a top-notch band and charismatic leadership both in the music and teaching. I thoroughly enjoyed myself except for two things. It was so dark in the room I could barely see my wife standing next to me. And for most of the music set, it was loud enough I could barely hear myself sing, let alone hear anyone not on mic in the band.

Neither of those things would have bothered me in a concert. But this was not a concert. This was an assembly of Christians gathered to worship together. That means we had certain obligations including that of teaching and building one another in the gospel through singing. A pitch-black room created an obstacle, as did the inability to hear my neighbors clearly all the way through. The lighting choices and the sound choices directed focus exclusively on the stage. This meant the band alone could carry out the biblical singing mandate to me and not vice-versa. How could I minister to my fellow Christians on stage or around me on the floor if they couldn't see or hear me?

Using lighting and sound to bring focus to the stage is important – how else can we coordinate our worship together? But the stage is a *means*, not an *end*. We must use our tools to draw the congregation in as *participants* rather than to wall them off as *spectators* or worse, *fans* (of us). The One we worship is not visibly on stage. He is in us and – particularly in corporate worship – *among* us.

Another issue that may impact your worship culture is the diversification of the community around you. You may find that your church population shifts over time from a homogeneous group to a diverse one, whether that relates to ethnicity, socio-economic status, age or other demographics. Such changes will probably mean that some shifts in your approach will be necessary, or at least should be considered.

Run in the Shoes

In addition to all the above, you will likely be confronted with leadership issues among the other musicians. Do you allow a non-Christian to play in the band? How much do you put up with a bad attitude or habitual tardiness or lack of preparation before addressing it, and *how* do you address it?

You will have to search out your own answers to these kinds of things. Generally, let me encourage you to aim for excellence, for naturally this honors God. Model personal preparation for those you lead. It should be evident that you have rehearsed and that you are constantly working to improve as a musician. Seek ways to help them improve too. Give them or help them discover tools they need to prepare. The resources are virtually endless, given all the online offerings these days. Be organized, and help them be organized.

Cultivate community over celebrity, both among your musicians and the crowd. Try to make the crowd forget the stage, to feel more like a part of the grand worship choir than like a spectator or concert-goer. They need to understand they serve you too in this gospel ministry. Worship leading is not something the band does *for* the church. It is something the band encourages the *whole church* to do together. To offset celebrity – and to provide variety – utilize different worship leaders as you are able. This is difficult in smaller churches with limited personnel, but you can still work against celebrity by having other capable singers take lead on vocals or even by backing off mic to emphasize the congregation's own collective voice as a sort of lead vocalist.

These are but a sampling of the many issues that impact how and whether your congregation will do what God has commanded when they gather to worship. As an influencer, as a leader, when you think these issues through, keep the main thing the main thing. There are a lot of ways to help the church build itself up on the true gospel together, but it only takes a misplaced priority or thoughtless tradition here or a careless cultural accommodation there to begin to unravel the whole fabric. Do your part in your ministry setting to not only stand in your gospel shoes, but to run in them. Reflect and innovate to make the most of those 75 minutes or so that you get to help direct your people's focus to their Savior at the finish line. If you are running on course, chances are they will be too.

Chapter 7: Challenge Others with the Shoes

I hope and pray that the Lord is causing these thoughts to resonate in your own situation and they will continue to spur you in your own journey as one who takes the stage. I could have spent more time digging into the many practical issues you will encounter, but I wanted to simply set you to thinking in terms of certain principles and categories. My approach has been to offer enough detail to illustrate those categories rather than to wear you out with anecdotes that may well be foreign to your own situations.

Now I want to urge you to take on the last important call of the shoes: transfer. Challenge others to put on the shoes. Do what I have been doing in this book. If God is stirring an awareness in you, an intimidating but compelling hunger, then respond to it. Understand that it must go further. You have been commanded to transfer that challenge to others. The reality of reproduction is built in to the Great Commission given to us by Jesus. His command to make disciples inherently includes the idea of transfer to the next generation of disciples, and the next, and the next, and so on. To become a disciple of Jesus is to become a disciple-*maker*. It is crucial for you to see *your* calling to wield your influence faithfully in the gospel shoes. It is just as important to see that you must help *others* see their own calling to their own shoes.

Think of it like a celebrity endorsement but much more. You may not see yourself as a celebrity (and it's good if you do not – ever!) but the first premise I offered in this book still stands. You do in fact have influence. Influence is the fundamental strategy behind celebrity endorsement: *I really appreciate and respect that person and their work, so if such and such is a big deal to them, then maybe it should be for me too.* In a really strong endorsement a celebrity may claim, "This really changed my life!" In truth, if you stand and kneel and run in your gospel shoes, you carry a much stronger message than that: "Jesus not only *changed* my life, he *gives* me life! He *is* my life!"

As you take on the shoes and find your fulfillment in the true gospel, your great opportunity and joy is to obey the command of Christ to recommend the shoes to others. You must leverage your influence and your platform to make others aware of their own calling to step into the shoes and begin to grow. How do you do that, when you may only be just beginning to realize your calling yourself?

Start by thinking in terms of your congregation. I have already shown that Scripture presents the gathered bodies of local congregations as having the responsibility of teaching. When your people gather to worship God, they are supposed to be teaching one another how to live by rehearsing the true gospel together. That is not your job alone or the preacher's job. It is everyone's job. Many of them do not realize this. Your great privilege is to stand in your shoes and tell them about their *own* sets of shoes. Just as you have influence, so do they, not only among their gathered brothers and sisters but out in the world of their daily lives. Just as you have a stage, so do they have a variety of platforms upon which to display the gospel at home, at work, at school – wherever they are. Challenge the congregants you serve to put on their gospel shoes.

Next, think about your bandmates, your singers, your technicians, the others you serve with and perhaps direct in your role on stage. There is a good chance they only see themselves in their technical roles: "I'm a singer," "I play some keys and some drums," "I do dramatic readings," or "I run the sound." There is a good chance they do not think of themselves as a worship leader, so they probably would not imagine that a pair of gospel shoes sits in front of them as I have described to you. Help them see their own shoes too. Show them the key role they have in influencing others with and for the gospel. This is how you serve them, and it is how you help them serve others – including serving you.

Challenge Others with the Shoes

Last, consider who might be gifted, called, and willing to have the kind of leadership role you may have. They may already be in your worship team, or they may show up soon as a new attender that expresses interest in joining your team. Part of growing and maturing in your own shoes is showing someone else theirs, and in particular you should look for someone that looks to have leadership chops. If you have been called to lead, then you have also been called to help someone else learn to lead. As any leadership trainer will tell you, that means approaching them about leadership and first giving them opportunities to learn from you while you lead. Then it means giving them chances to lead in limited ways while you support, and finally handing off to them some leadership responsibilities to hold on their own.

For example, if you see a bandmate that seems to have leadership potential, have a conversation about the possibility. If they are open to it, start with having them lead a song. Help them give direction to the band. Encourage them and give them tips. If they do well, maybe let them help you select songs for an upcoming set and lead part of it. Eventually, you can have them plan and lead a service, and help them learn from what worked and what didn't as you reflect upon it later.

Only you can figure out what this handoff looks like in your context. My point is that the calling to the shoes that I have tried to pass on to you must pass on *from* you to someone *else*. As many as possible. That's my heart, and it's why I'm writing a book – to try to maximize the spreading of this challenge to as many worship leaders as possible. I have only been around a limited number of potential worship leaders in my own church environments. I've certainly missed some opportunities to pass on this challenge, but I have worked harder over recent years to pour into others, to elevate their understanding of the gravity and privilege of leading congregational worship. God has given me a passion for this that is bigger than my own context, so I seek to spread the word. Hence, a book.

I realize that sGod is sovereign over my influence, as he is yours. I simply want to maximize my influence for this important cause, and I want you to maximize yours. It has long been noted that gospel ministry is one of multiplication. Perhaps only one person will read this book and catch the fire of God for gospel ministry – *you*. So be it. Perhaps you will grab the attention of several others and transfer the passion of the shoes to them. Sweet! My prayer is that whatever part I play, however limited, the eventual result is exponentially greater. May God raise up a generation of worship leaders who understand both their influence and their responsibility, who leverage that responsibility to bring gospel life into our churches. If he will, it will come through awareness, willingness, and commitment.

To that end, I'll say it again: you have influence by nature of your position on the stage. Your influence may well grow, because God has placed you in that position. I have been charged with helping you realize the responsibility that comes with this influence. You have big shoes to step into. That's not quite the cliché – "big shoes to *fill*" – and for good reason. These shoes are branded by the true gospel. If you own up to your responsibility, you do not fill these shoes. They fill *you*. Your challenge to step into the shoes is to be filled with gospel truth. Your call to grow in the shoes is to grow in the gospel, in awareness, understanding, and obedience. Your mandate to kneel in the shoes is Jesus' mandate to perform gospel ministry that is patterned after his own – a ministry of loving service to others. Your call to stand in the shoes is to anchor yourself in the gospel, to guard it and to rest in it as the framework for your own identity and that of the ministry to which God has called you. Your challenge to run in the shoes is to continually translate the gospel into diverse and changing contexts, staying fixated on Christ with a firm footing in the changeless content of truth while you discern the flexible and suitable expressions of that content.

Challenge Others with the Shoes

At the risk of overextending my clothing metaphor, let me point out that you will need to wear a number of hats that come with your skinny jeans. Your assigned practical role may seem limited in scope – maybe only to lead the singing, maybe more. But if you step into the shoes, and grow and kneel and stand and run, then you wear the hat of a theologian, a disciple, a witness, a steward, a shepherd, a servant, a devotee, even a consultant.

Here's the beautiful thing about the gospel shoes. If you answer the calling God has set before you, the gospel will both unsettle you and settle you. On one hand, you will never be fully satisfied with the gospel work you are attempting to do for the Savior to whom you keep pressing forward. On the other hand, you will be able to reflect in any given moment and realize that God is *fully* satisfied with you in Christ and is being faithful to complete this work in you until you are finally face to face with him.

Skinny jeans, bell-bottoms, robes, tees, tassels, sweaters, dresses, or three-piece suits; country, gospel, country-gospel, pop-rock, acoustic, electric, synth, folk, orchestral, or a cappella; stained glass, clear glass, no glass, no building, candles, chandeliers, screens or hymnals... To summarize from Jesus, "Heaven and earth will pass away, but my words will never pass away." You are immersed in your moment, and a thousand things will demand your attention. Most of them will be attached to what I have represented with the symbol of the skinny jeans. They will pass away because they are not the substance of your calling. *That* you will find symbolized in the shoes.

The gospel calls you. It calls you to Jesus. On the way it calls you to the people he loves enough that he died for them. Step into his shoes. Grow into them. Kneel in them. Stand in them. Run in them. Challenge others to do the same.

1 Corinthians 9:24–27

Don't you know that the runners in a stadium all race, but only one receives the prize? Run in such a way to win the prize. Now everyone who competes exercises self-control in everything. They do it to receive a perishable crown, but we an imperishable crown. So I do not run like one who runs aimlessly or box like one beating the air. Instead, I discipline my body and bring it under strict control, so that after preaching to others, I myself will not be disqualified.

www.ingramcontent.com/pod-product-compliance
Lightning Source LLC
Chambersburg PA
CBHW031451070426
42452CB00038B/792